STEM Jobs in Food and Nutrition

Jane Katirgis

rourkeeducationalmedia.com

Before Reading:

Building Academic Vocabulary and Background Knowledge

Before reading a book, it is important to tap into what your child or students already know about the topic. This will help them develop their vocabulary, increase their reading comprehension, and make connections across the curriculum.

1. *Look at the cover of the book. What will this book be about?*
2. *What do you already know about the topic?*
3. *Let's study the Table of Contents. What will you learn about in the book's chapters?*
4. *What would you like to learn about this topic? Do you think you might learn about it from this book? Why or why not?*
5. *Use a reading journal to write about your knowledge of this topic. Record what you already know about the topic and what you hope to learn about the topic.*
6. *Read the book.*
7. *In your reading journal, record what you learned about the topic and your response to the book.*
8. *After reading the book complete the activities below.*

Content Area Vocabulary
Read the list. What do these words mean?

abundance
bacteria
biotechnology
cholesterol
chromatography
contaminated
fermentation
gene
genetically-modified food
microbes
preservative
sanitary
saturated fat
specialized

After Reading:

Comprehension and Extension Activity

After reading the book, work on the following questions with your child or students in order to check their level of reading comprehension and content mastery.

1. *Describe the role of STEM in the food industry. (Summarize)*
2. *Why might some farmers choose not to spray their crops with pesticides? (Infer)*
3. *How do you benefit from preservatives used in food? (Text to self connection)*
4. *Describe the role of technology in agriculture. (Summarize)*
5. *How do CDC scientists track an outbreak? (Visualize)*

Extension Activity

Where does your food come from? Write down all of the ingredients in your lunch today. Research what states or countries produce the majority of this food. Create a map showing where everything in your lunch came from.

Table of Contents

What does STEM stand for?

Science
Technology
Engineering
Mathematics

What Is STEM?

Sit down at your dinner table and take a look at the food in front of you. It may seem simple, but in reality, many people are hard at work making the food we eat every day. Food chemists create new flavors for packaged food. Farmers calculate the number of seeds to buy for planting all their fields. Dietitians use nutritional software programs to plan diets for people with food allergies.

All these people make a living working in jobs that require a STEM education. STEM is a quick way of talking about science, technology, engineering, and mathematics.

Some of the most exciting careers are in STEM fields. A strong STEM education can take you to the next level in just about any career field. What great STEM job may be waiting for you?

A scientist records his observations of a crop of corn.

Chemistry and Food

When is the last time you had ethyl butyrate? If you drank orange juice at breakfast, you probably had some of this added flavor this morning!

Years ago, families shopped each day for fresh food. Today businesses make products, such as packaged orange juice, that last weeks in a refrigerator or months when it is unopened. But to do this, they have to take out parts that can cause it to go bad quickly. But this also removes some flavor. A flavor chemist supplies new flavors, such as ethyl butyrate, to add back to the juice.

A flavor chemist creates many flavors to add to packaged food.

Flavor chemists study the chemicals that give foods their unique flavor, such as sweet strawberry or savory roasted tomato. Then they mix pure forms of these chemicals, hoping to recreate the flavor so that a food company will use it.

Food scientists also study how flavors interact with each other. How does freezing or heating affect the flavor? A raspberry flavor used in a liquid sports drink might not be as delicious in a cookie mix if it breaks down during baking.

STEM in Action!

Testing Your Taste

Which of your senses do you think is most important when identifying a flavor? You can do an experiment to find out.

Cut a small piece of peeled potato and a small piece of peeled apple into equal sizes. Place each on a plate. Close your eyes and hold your nose. Ask a partner to feed you one piece without telling you if it is the apple or potato. Keep holding your nose and try the second piece. Can you tell the difference?

Do you think your sense of smell is as important as your sense of taste in identifying flavors?

Food scientists also improve ways to can, freeze, and package foods while keeping them flavorful and safe. Some research new food sources, such as seaweed. Others work on engineering new packaging to keep cookies crisp. No one wants to eat a soggy cookie!

STEM Fast Fact:

Food scientists may work in laboratories that are set up like kitchens. They use blenders, ovens, and other cooking equipment.

Foods like tuna fish and soup can be packaged in cans. Scientists keep improving ways to make canned food taste fresh.

Real STEM Job: *Food Engineer*

When ketchup flows out of a bottle, it makes a great topping for a hamburger. But why doesn't it swish out quickly like water or glop out slowly like honey? Food engineers create the proper flow and thickness of products, based on how the foods need to act. So for ketchup, they know that it needs to break off easily from the bottle at the end of pouring. Also, it should not drip off of the hamburger.

Food engineers also work on something called mouth feel, which is how food feels in your mouth. The creaminess of peanut butter or the chewiness of bread influences how people feel about their food.

The creamy, rich texture of chocolate makes it a favorite food of many people.

The Numbers in Nutrition

Foods contain different amounts of carbohydrates, proteins, fats, vitamins, minerals, and calories. How many of each does a person need every day? How does the right amount of food keep a person healthy or treat disease? Finding these things out is all part of a nutritionist's day at work.

A nutritionist may work with someone who has high cholesterol or diabetes. The nutritionist teaches the person which foods have high amounts of cholesterol. Then, he or she explains how the amount of sugar in food affects a person's blood sugar level. Then, the nutritionist will create a diet especially for the person. The diet will include how many times a day to eat and which foods to avoid.

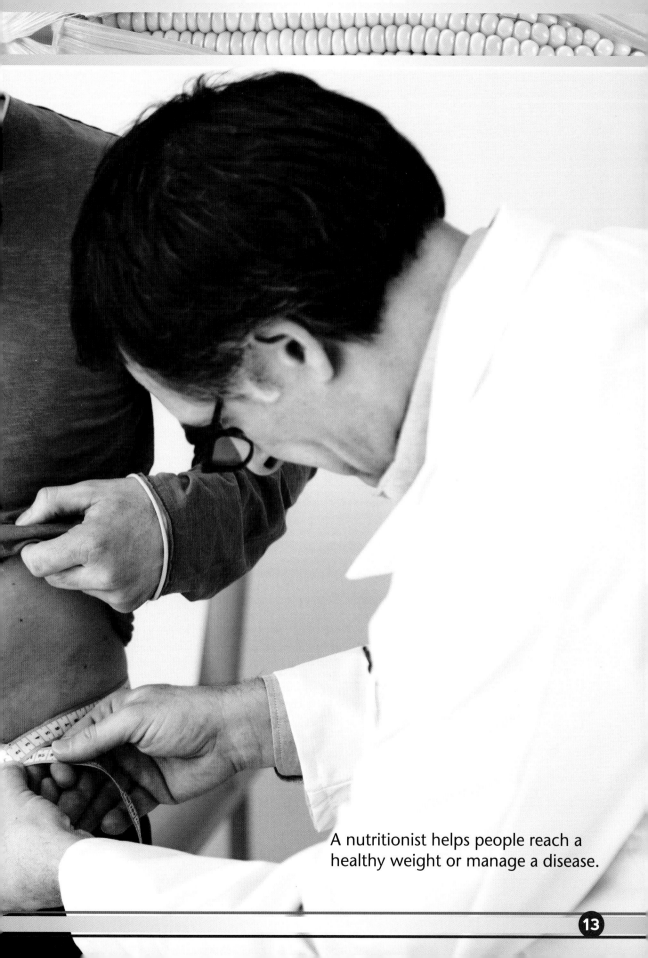

A nutritionist helps people reach a healthy weight or manage a disease.

STEM in Action!

How Many Calories Are in a Meal?

You are hungry. You sit down to a full plate and get ready to dig in. You are probably thinking about how good your food will taste, not about math! But all the food on your plate is full of different numbers.

Let's look at a dinner that contains 3 ounces of roasted chicken, one large roasted sweet potato with a tablespoon of butter, and 1 cup of broccoli. And wash it down with a cup of low fat milk.

1 large sweet potato: 162 calories
1 tablespoon butter: 102 calories
3 ounces chicken: 190 calories
1 cup broccoli: 54 calories
1 cup low fat milk: 105 calories

How many calories does your dinner have?

Add the calories from each item:

162 + 102 + 190 + 54 + 105 = 613

Your dinner has 613 calories.

Many nutritionists work for a government agency, such as the U.S. Department of Agriculture (USDA). They make the nutritional rules for school lunch programs. They decide what amounts of protein, fat, and other nutrients are just right for kids' meals.

Perhaps you have noticed the Nutrition Facts labels on packaged food. The labels list serving size and calories. Government nutritionists at the Federal Department of Agriculture (FDA) are in charge of the standards on these labels. They decide what percent of your daily diet (listed as % dietary value) should be made up of **saturated fat** or sugar.

Real STEM Job:
Registered Dietitian

Some registered dietitians work at hospitals and nursing homes. They create meal plans for many different patients. Heart patients need diets low in saturated fats, so they will not be eating red meat for lunch and dinner. Patients with high blood pressure will be given low-sodium diets, which means their soups and other meal choices will not have added salt. The dietitian works with the doctors to plan meals that meet a patient's nutritional needs.

Sometimes hospital dietitians not only plan the menus, but also manage the entire food service department. They oversee the budget for buying the food and supplies for all the meals. That's a lot of number crunching!

Dietitians make sure each hospital patient gets just the right food.

Animals Need Good Food, Too

Most nutritionists and dietitians work to keep people healthy. But who is in charge of keeping animals on healthy diets? That is the job of an animal nutritionist.

Perhaps you have a pet at home: a playful dog, a colorful parakeet, or even a pot-bellied pig. Pet nutrition companies hire scientists to create **specialized** pet foods. They work in laboratories, combining ingredients like master chefs for pets. They perform studies to make sure the pets like the taste. Because a food won't be very nutritious if the animal won't eat it!

Before a pet enjoys its customized food, many scientists have worked to make it healthy, tasty, and safe.

Engineers and scientists work with machines to create different forms of food. For example, dog food can be sold as dry, semi-moist nuggets, bone-shaped treats, or premium mixes. Each has a different density, texture, shape, and color. And they all need to be made in cost-effective, **sanitary** ways.

STEM in Action!

How Do Pet Foods Compare?

Look at two or more pet food ingredient labels. If you don't have a pet, maybe your friend does. Or you can visit the supermarket and look at the pet food labels there.

For example, look at the ingredient labels of dry dog food and dry cat food. The first item listed is the ingredient present in the highest amount in the food. What is the first item listed for dog and cat food? How do the number of ingredients compare?

Now compare dry dog food with wet, canned dog food. What differences do you see on these labels?

Without proper nutrition, a racehorse will not be in its best shape.

A mere second can be the difference between the Triple Crown and second place. Some animal nutritionists help feed racehorses so that they have the energy to perform their best.

Researchers are improving ways for racehorses to get the vitamins they need for healthy muscles. They invented a patch that the horse can wear on its skin. The horse absorbs the chemicals, which improve the effect of the vitamins they're given.

Real STEM Job: *Zoo Nutritionist*

Animal nutritionists who work on zoo diets have the most varied nutrition careers of all. There are so many animals at the zoo! Some critters eat just insects, some eat only meat, and others eat grass and leaves. That's a lot of different menus.

Zoo nutritionists use computer programs to figure out how much fat, protein, carbohydrates, vitamins, and minerals each unique species needs. They plan menus with the zookeepers to provide these nutrients.

Some companies, like Purina, hire scientists to create monkey chow, elephant chow, polar bear chow, and more! Zoo nutritionists work with the scientists to create ready-to-eat packaged food that is perfect for each species. They match the level of nutrients in an animal's natural, wild diet. The shape of the food needs to be just right, too. For example, feed for anteaters is shaped for slurping through their tube-shaped mouths.

Anteater

A zoo nutritionist may feed these Macaque corn.

Agriculture and the Farm

Where does all our food come from? You might be clever and say, "the supermarket," but how does it get there? To feed the growing population, agricultural scientists help farmers grow, harvest, and process an **abundance** of high-quality foods.

Biotechnology companies are working on **genetically-modified** (GM) foods that have genes from other species inserted into them. The inserted genes help the plant do something the scientist wants. It may help the plant fight disease or be unharmed by a chemical.

There is a GM corn that has a **gene** from a bacterium inserted into it. This bacterium makes a natural pesticide. When a pesky corn borer insect munches on the GM corn, the bug gets a hole in its gut and dies.

If you hear the term *space-age farming*, you may imagine growing tomatoes on Mars. But farmers on Earth now use satellite images taken from space to check the health of their plants and soil.

The satellites sense the energy of everything on Earth and make pictures. These fascinating images show the difference between healthy and stressed plants. The images help farmers figure out whether their plants need more water or if they have been given too much fertilizer.

The satellite photo on the left shows the true color of farmland. The same farm is imaged in infrared on the right, showing healthy crops (red), areas of flooding (black), and unwanted pesticides (brown).

STEM in Action!

Temperature and Food Quality

When most crops are picked, they need to be kept cool so that they stay fresh. Engineers develop high-speed cooling equipment and refrigerated buildings to store crops immediately after picking. You can do an experiment to test how temperature affects lettuce quality.

Take a few leaves of lettuce from the same head. Place two leaves in the refrigerator and two leaves on a dish in the cabinet. This way, light conditions are the same for both: dark. Which leaves wilt faster? How important do you think temperature is when trucks ship lettuce across the country?

Once the food makes it to the store shelf, a shopper may wonder: Where did that peach come from? Were the eggs shipped from far away? Is the cheese packaging recyclable? Computer programmers are inventing smartphone technology so that a shopper can scan a food label. Blip! Then the shopper will be able to see what farm grew the food, when it was picked, how long it has been on the store shelf, and whether it is organic.

Smartphone technology will tell shoppers about the farm that grew the food.

STEM Spotlight: Robots in the Field

There is a lot of hard field work to be done once a crop is ready to be picked, especially if it does not all ripen at the same time. Workers have to carefully pick only the ripe fruits and vegetables. How about getting a robot to do some of the work?

Agricultural engineers have invented robots that can pick ripe lettuce or strawberries. A camera on the robot creates a 3D image of the strawberry. A program analyzes the photos and determines whether the berry is ripe enough to pick. The robot can snip the strawberry from the vine and place it in a padded container in nine seconds.

Sensors allow the robot to check the color, quality, and size of a fruit so that it only picks ripe fruit.

Harvesting crops, like these carrots, is hard work for humans. Robots can help make it easier!

Food Safety Technology

Our food comes from all over the world: beef from Nebraska, fruit from Chile, and juice squeezed in China. USDA inspectors make sure that all food is safe to eat. Harmful pesticides or disease-causing **microbes** are not welcome guests at the dinner table.

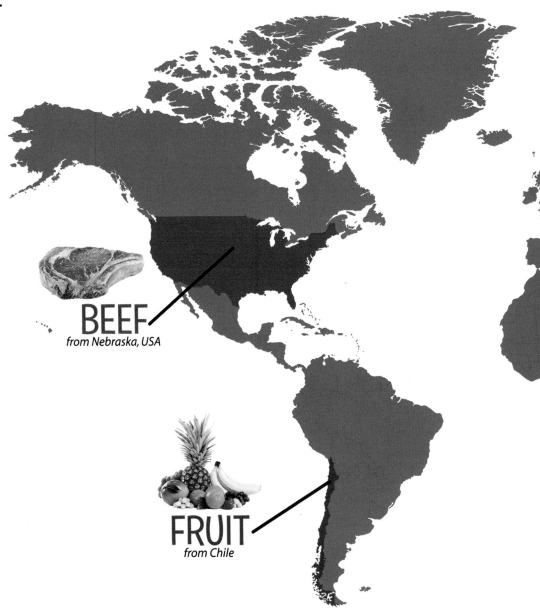

BEEF
from Nebraska, USA

FRUIT
from Chile

Biotechnology scientists design small, handheld devices to test meat quickly before it is packaged for the store. These sensors can test for six different types of bacteria that could make a person sick. The results are ready in about an hour. Older tests took up to three days to give results.

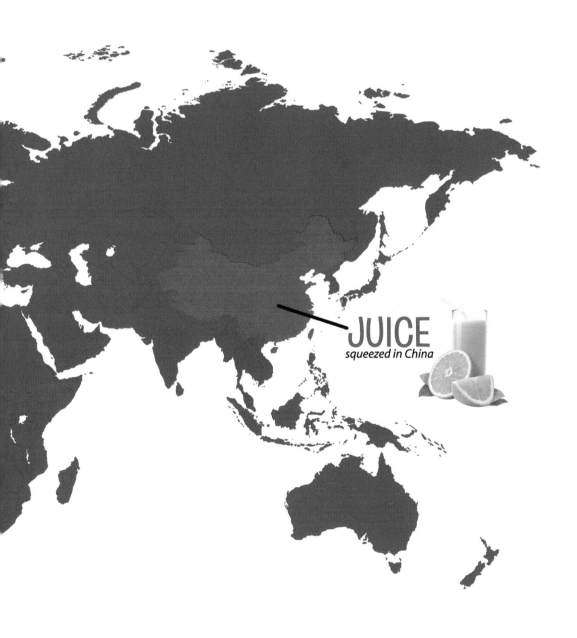

JUICE
squeezed in China

STEM in Action!

Where Is Your Food Coming From?

For one day, take a closer look at every food item you eat. Write down what country the food came from. Fresh fruit and vegetables will have a sticker or label that says "product of USA" or "product of Chile." Packaged food often has the country of origin on the label also.

At the end of the day, make a chart like this:

Country	Number of Food Items
United States	6
Chile	4
Canada	1
Mexico	4

How many items came from the United States? What percent of your food came from another country? To calculate the percent, let's look at the example above:

Total food items listed: 6 + 4 + 1 + 4 = 15

Total food from outside the U.S.: 4 + 1 + 4 = 9

Percent of food from outside the U.S.:
9 ÷ 15 = 0.6, or 60 percent

Some food chemists use **chromatography** machines to separate the many parts of a food sample. These machines can measure even the smallest amount of disease-causing bacteria or illegal pesticides.

Scientists test samples from different foods to make sure that farmers and food manufacturers are delivering safe food to market.

Real STEM Job:

CDC Food Outbreak Surveillance Scientist

    Salmonella. . . *E. coli* . . . *Listeria* . . . These are scary microbes in the world of food. Food that is **contaminated** with these nasty bacteria can make people very sick. If mystery, science, and math are some of your favorite topics, then you just might have the right skills to be a food outbreak detective.

Salmonella bacteria, magnified 3,200 times.

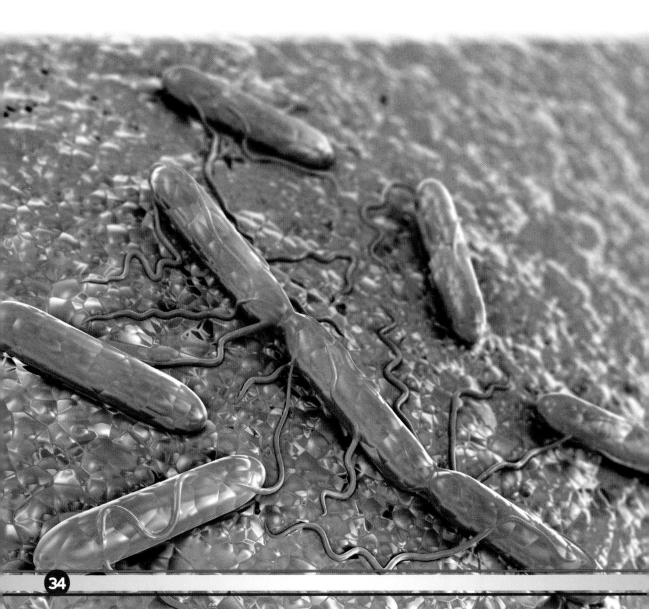

The CDC is a government agency in Atlanta, Georgia.

When a group of people is thought to have foodborne illness, the local health department contacts the Centers for Disease Control and Prevention (CDC). Government scientists get to work. They investigate who, what, when, where, and why: Who got sick? What did they eat? When did they first get sick? Where did the food come from? Why are they sick? They use science and math, along with sharp problem-solving skills, to track the outbreak.

These scientists are also good communicators. They talk with other scientists and doctors, notify the public, and work with restaurants, supermarkets, and food suppliers to solve the mystery of where the contaminated food came from.

Microbiology and Food

Cheese and fresh baked bread sound like the makings of a satisfying snack. But how these foods are made is all a matter of science! Many common foods and drinks are created when microbes are part of the mix. But don't worry, although some microbes can cause disease, most are harmless. And many are helpful! Food microbiologists are trained to know the difference.

Makers of cheese, pickles, yogurt, beer, and wine need microbiologists to help them keep fermented products at their best. **Fermentation** occurs when yeast and bacteria change sugar to acid (when making cheese), gas (to make bread rise), or alcohol (to create wine and beer).

STEM Fast Fact:

Scientists may be in charge of making sure a vat of wine is not spoiled by bad bacteria. Or they may work to improve yogurt products with good bacteria that make people healthier. These scientists have great senses of smell, too. Some of them can sniff out the difference between six types of bacteria!

STEM in Action!

Yeast is a fungus that is often packaged and used to make bread and other foods.

But how does this work? To find out how temperature affects yeast, add half a package of yeast to two separate bowls. Add very warm water to one bowl and ice cold water to the second bowl. Watch to see how quickly and how many bubbles appear.

Do you think the temperature of the water affects how quickly dough will rise?

Bakery scientists also study the yeast reactions that occur during baking. They design and test new baking mixes. Perhaps it is a sandwich bread mix or a microwavable hot pretzel recipe. The scientists use math skills to figure out the best combination of ingredients in these mixes.

Bakers see science in action with every batch of bread they bake!

STEM Fast Fact:

If you like organic food, you are not the only one! More and more people want to eat food that is grown without chemicals. Organic farmers study the tiny microbes that live in the soil. Healthy soil means healthy crops and much less need for chemicals.

Real STEM Job: *Cheese Microbiologist*

Without very specific microbes, your cheese would simply be milk! Cheese makers first add bacteria to curdle milk into a solid chunk. Then they add bacteria and mold to help give the cheese its unique flavor, color, and texture. Cheese microbiologists study how different bacteria and mold result in different tastes and textures of cheese.

Milk is curdled in a cheese factory.

Companies such as Land O'Lakes hire microbiologists to hunt for the microbes that can create new cheeses. They also work on making the companies' cheese recipes better. For example, the scientist may work on a project for a pizza company that wants its cheese to have just the right stretch. It also has to brown the right amount during cooking, and of course have the perfect melt.

Improving Nutrition

Back in the old days, people cured some meat, canned some food, stored some potatoes, and hoped they had enough food to make it through the winter. Today, thanks to food scientists, there are many different food products available on supermarket shelves. Even during the coldest months, **preservatives** make it possible for you to enjoy fruits and vegetables from around the world. And because scientists calculate the nutritional value in food, when you enjoy a hunk of cheese, you know exactly how many calories you are eating.

The careers involved in food, nutrition, agriculture, and cooking are varied and exciting. Whether you love to do research, learn about nutrition, or design the latest technology for agriculture, you will find that STEM skills are essential in getting to a dream career. So curl up with a healthy snack, open that science book, and dig in!

STEM Job Fact Sheets

Agricultural Engineer

Important Skills: Mathematics, Science, Computers, Problem-Solving

Important Knowledge: Agriculture, Biology, Mathematics, Engineering, Technology

College Major: Agricultural Engineering, Biological Engineering

Median Salary: $71,090

Flavor Chemist

Important Skills: Creativity, Mathematics, Science, Good Sense of Smell and Taste, Good Odor Memory

Important Knowledge: Flavor Characteristics, Chemistry

College Major: Chemistry, Biology, Food Science

Median Salary: $69,790*

*data provided is for chemist

Food Microbiologist

Important Skills: Biology, Science, Microscopy, Manual Dexterity in the Laboratory

Important Knowledge: Biology, Science, Food, Health, Statistics

College Major: Biology, Microbiology, Food Science

Median Salary: $65,920*

*data provided is for microbiologist

Food Safety Specialist

Important Skills: Problem-Solving, Observation, Business, Science, Mathematics

Important Knowledge: Health, Microbiology

College Major: Biology, Chemistry, Food Science, Microbiology

Median Salary: $64,660*

*data provided is for occupational health and safety specialists

Registered Dietitian

Important Skills: Mathematics, Science, Health

Important Knowledge: Nutrition, Mathematics, Food Groups, Biology, Health

College Major: Biology, Chemistry, Nursing

Median Salary: $53,250

Zoo Nutritionist

Important Skills: Communication, Science, Health, Computer Databases

Important Knowledge: Animal Physiology, Nutrition, Biology, Zoology, Chemistry

College Major: Biology, Zoology, Chemistry, Animal Science, Biochemistry

Median Salary: $55,000

Glossary

abundance (uh-BUHN-duhns): having a great supply of something

bacteria (bak-TEER-ee-uh): microscopic, single-celled organisms that live in water, soil, animals, and plants

biotechnology (bye-oh-tek-NAH-luh-jee): using living organisms in manufacturing or other business

cholesterol (koh-LES-ter-ol): a compound found in an animal's body, including humans

chromatography (kroh-muh-TAH-gruh-fee): a technique done in a laboratory that separates mixtures

contaminated (kuhn-TAM-uh-nay-tid): something that has been made unsafe by the addition of a harmful substance

fermentation (fer-men-TAY-shun): a process in which yeast and bacteria change sugar to gas, alcohol, or acid

gene (JEEN): a piece of DNA that is passed from parent to offspring

genetically-modified (juh-NE-tik-lee MAH-di-fyed): describing a food or organism that has been artificially changed by adding genes from another species, giving it a desired characteristic

microbes (MYE-krobes): a very small living things that cannot be seen without a microscope

preservative (pri-ZURV-uh-tiv): something that keeps food fresh longer

sanitary (SAN-i-ter-ee): clean and free of germs or harmful bacteria

saturated fat (SA-chur-ay-tid FAT): an animal or vegetable fat that is solid at room temperature and can cause high cholesterol levels in the blood

specialized (SPESH-uh-lized): focused on a particular subject or need

Index

Show What You Know

1. What technology allows farmers to assess the health of their crops from space?
2. Why do flavor chemists make ingredients for packaged foods?
3. How do animal nutritionists know what to feed captive animals in the zoo?
4. What could make food unsafe to eat?
5. What careers involve dietary guidelines and menu planning?

Websites to Visit

http://www.coolsciencecareers.rice.edu

http://www.engineergirl.org

http://www.tryscience.org

About the Author

Jane Katirgis lives in an old farmhouse where she enjoys growing food and cooking for her friends and family. Her love of science and nature led her to a BS degree in biology and an MS degree in environmental science. She is a children's science book editor and author, and an Etsy shop owner. She lives in New Jersey with her husband, John, and their four egg-laying chickens.

Meet The Author!
www.meetREMauthors.com

PHOTO CREDITS: Cover © mediaphotos, luchschen, anyalvanova, BreatheFitness Image in header bars © Maks Narodenko; Title Page © stockyimages; Page 4 © Christian Draghici, page 5 © Goodluz; page 6 © Fineart1, page 7 top © revers, page 7 bottom © Africa Studio; page 8 left © Valentina Proskurina, right © Feng Yu, page 9 © Tomas Jasinskis; page 10 © Melica, page 11 © Christo; page 12-13 © Image Point Fr; page 15 © Brian A Jackson; page 16-17 © Monkey Business Images; page 18 and page 19 top © Goodluz, page 19 bottom © Africa Studio; page 20 left © Denniro, right antpkr, page 21 © Cheryl Ann Quigley; page 22 © weerayut ranmai, page 23 © Eric Isselee; page 24-25 © Marcin Balcerzak, page NASA Earth Observatory, Jesse Allen; page 26 © SeDmi, page 27 © 06photo; page 28 © Max Lindenthaler, page 28-29 © spirit of america; page 33 © Alex011973; page 34 © MichaelTaylor3d, page 35 photo © Katherine Welles; page 36-37 © Mariusz Szczygiel, page 37 top © Givaga; page 38 © ChameleonsEye, page 39 © wavebreakmedia; page 40 © MatthiasKabel, page 41 top © Valentyn Volkov, bottom © Denis Vrublevski; page 42 © Aleksandar Mijatovic, page 43 © Singkham

Edited by: Jill Sherman

Cover design by: Tara Raymo
Interior design by: Nicola Stratford   www.nicolastratford.com

Library of Congress PCN Data

STEM Jobs in Food and Nutrition / Jane Katirgis
(STEM Jobs You'll Love)
 ISBN 978-1-62717-703-0 (hard cover)
 ISBN 978-1-62717-825-9 (soft cover)
 ISBN 978-1-62717-939-3 (e-Book)
Library of Congress Control Number: 2014935497

Printed in the United States of America, North Mankato, Minnesota

Also Available as: